Christmas Coloring
Fun for All

Suzanna Stinnett
2015

Published by Coloring Camelot

Copyright 2015 Suzanna Stinnett

All rights reserved.

ISBN-10: 0692521720
ISBN-13: 978-0692521724 (Coloring Camelot)

This playful Christmas coloring book
is dedicated to the creative imagination in
each of us. It is designed for family time together
during the holidays. I hope it brings peace
and comfort to your holiday table.

Inside:

Christmas images for all skill levels!
Thumb through and find the simplest ones
for easy coloring, as well as more complex images
for the coloring enthusiast in your home!

WRAPPING PAPER!

The second half of this book contains sheets which are
meant to be colored, cut out of the book, and used as
wrapping paper for your smaller packages this Christmas.
Each image has three pages, which you can tape together
for a larger wrapping. Color them just as you like.
This is a unique way to express
your special regard for your beloveds.

Merry Christmas and a peaceful New Year!

Suzanna Stinnett

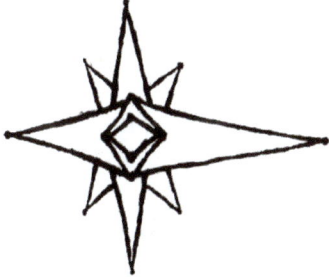

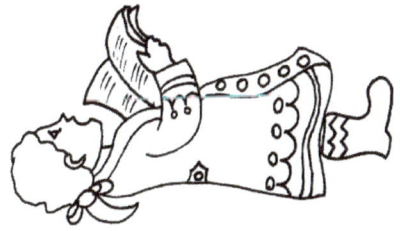

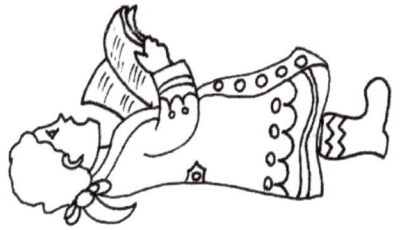

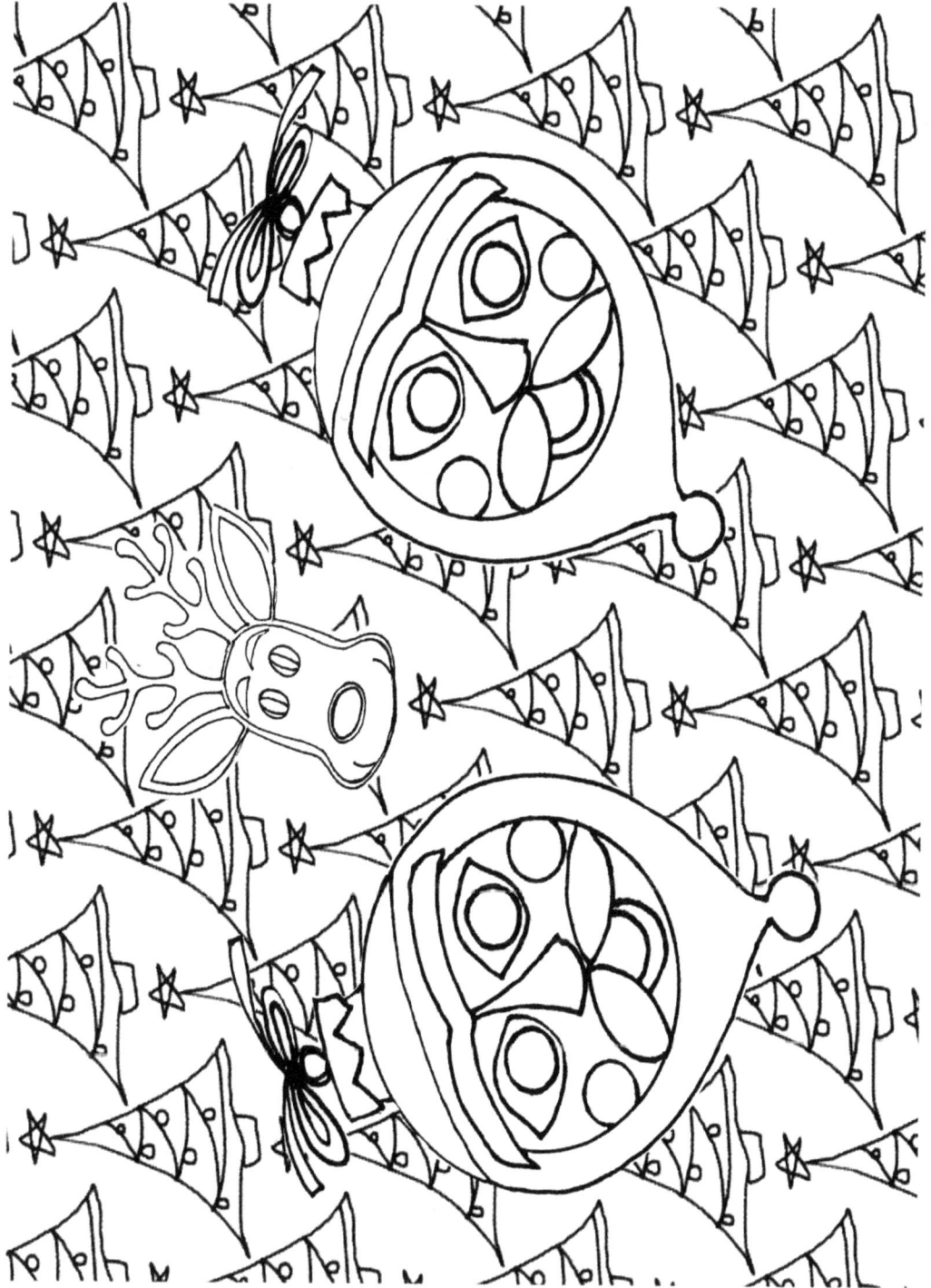

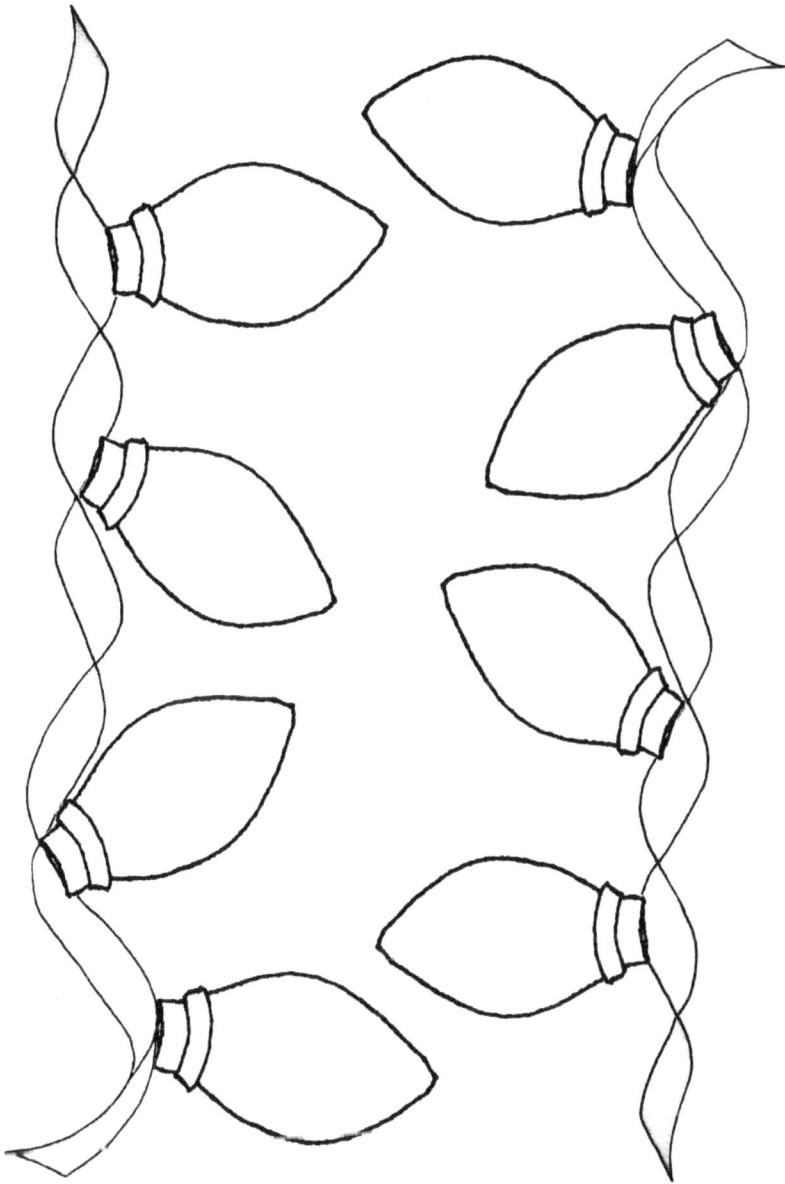

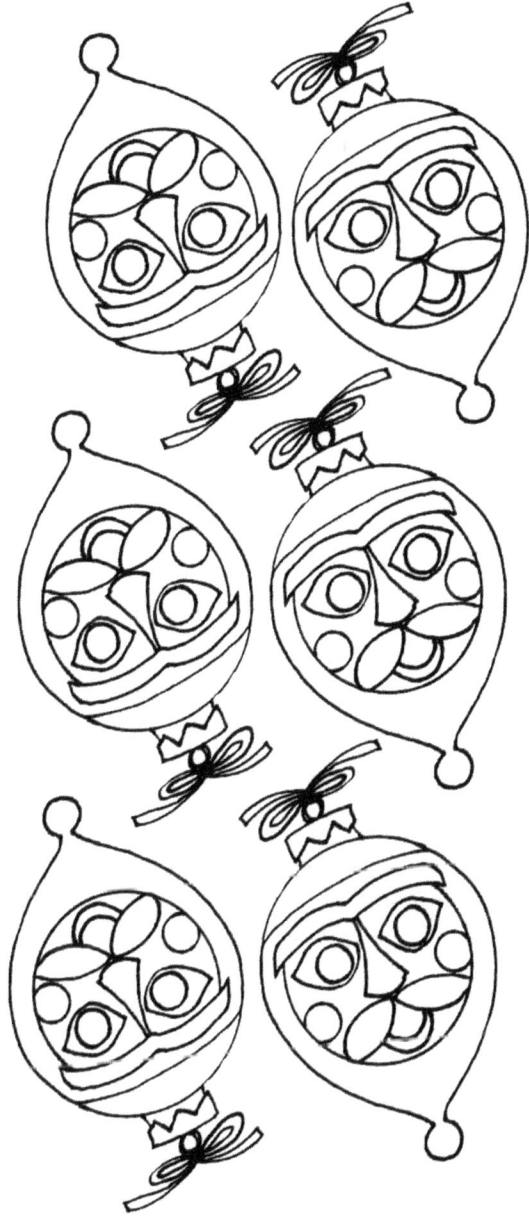

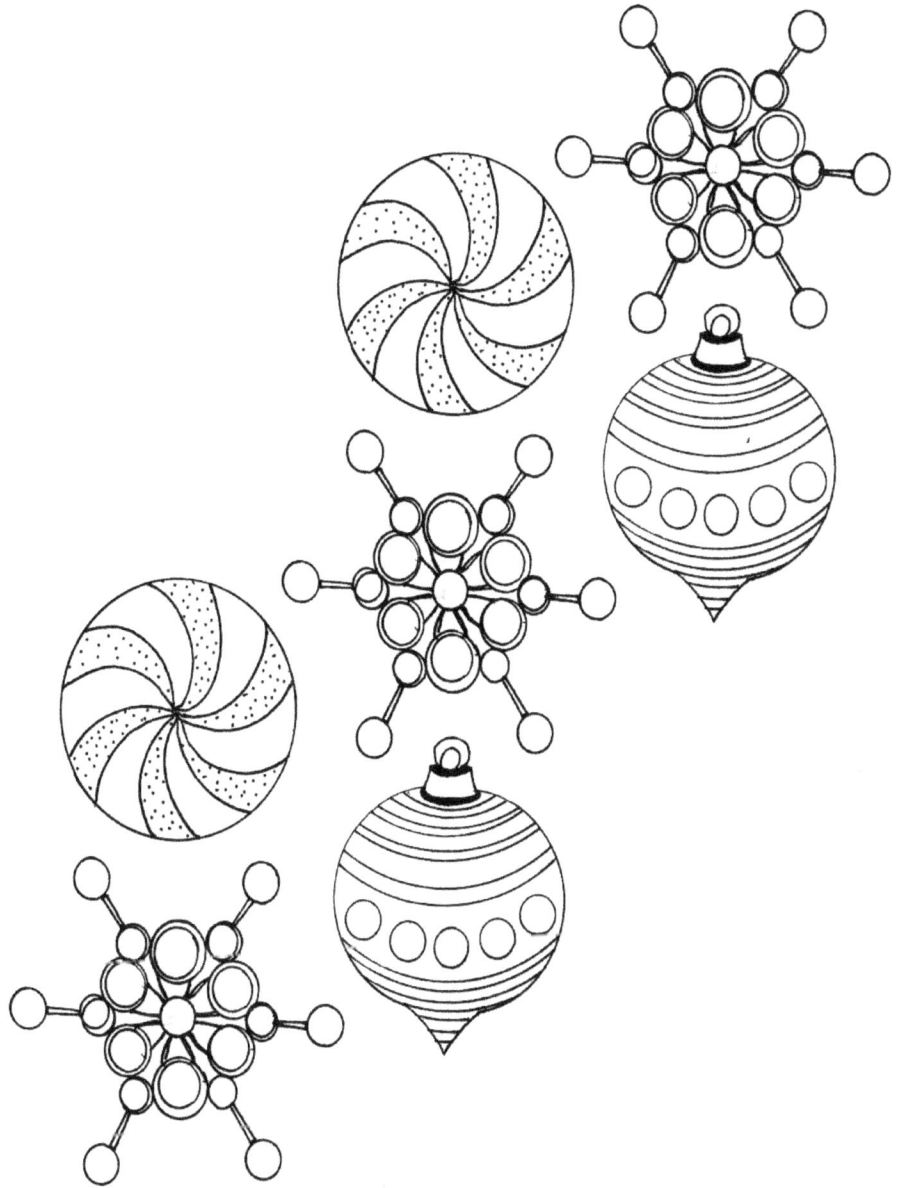

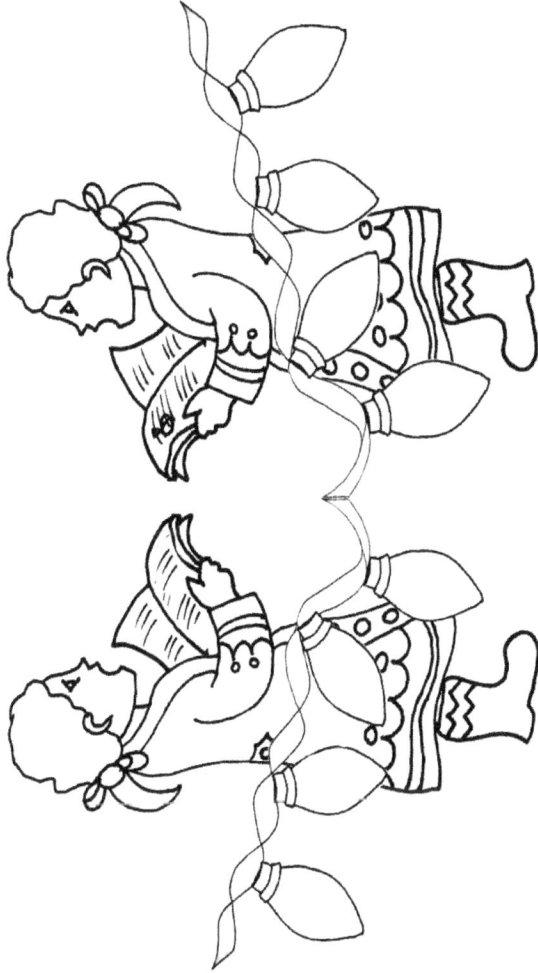

The second half of Christmas Coloring Fun for All
is designed to work as wrapping paper!

Each design has three pages.
Color them all the same,
Or make each one different!

To cut the sheets from the book,
open the book out flat.
Press on both sides of the book to flatten more.
Take a butter knife and press a line
into the edge near the binding.
Let the binding guide you to make
a sharp dent in the paper.
Now, hold the butter knife against the paper,
and tear gently to remove.

You can also use an X-Acto knife
to cut a crisper line along the edge.
Just be sure you use it safely!!!

You can also copy these designs on your copy machine.
Tape them together to wrap larger packages!

Have fun making your own wrapping paper!

Simple designs are also included.
Everyone can color their own!

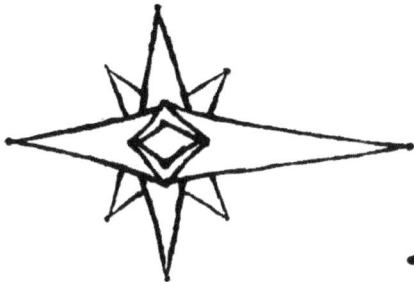

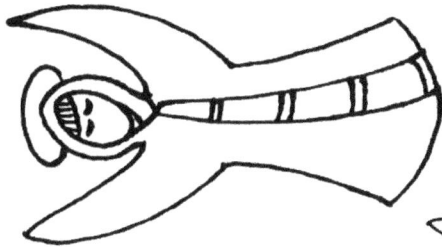

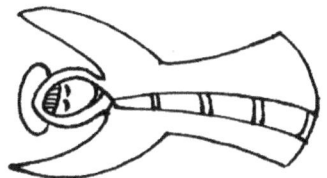

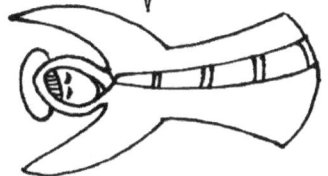

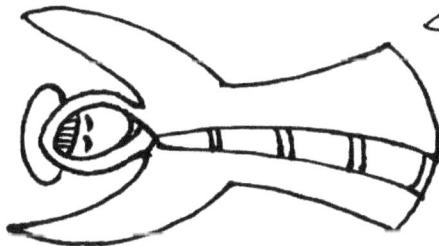

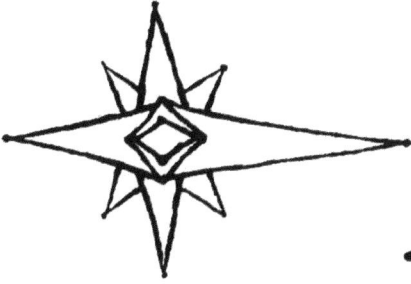

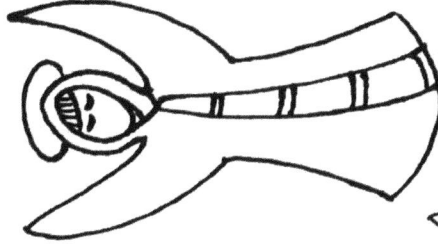

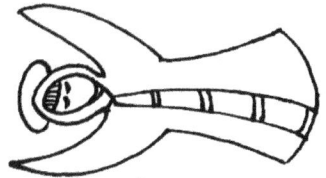

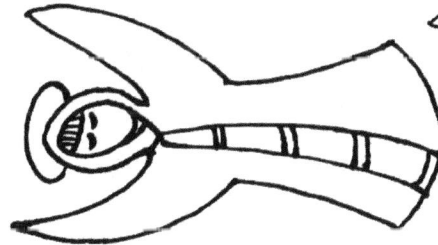

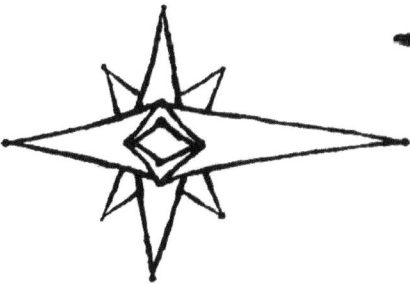

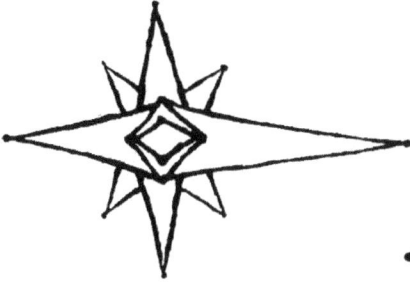

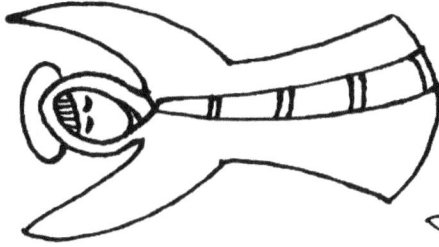

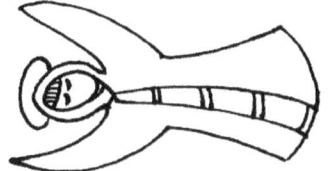

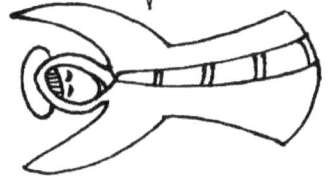

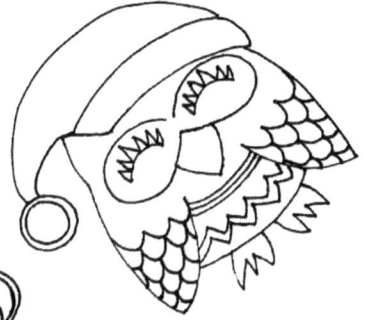

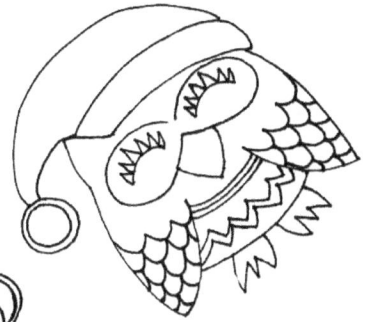

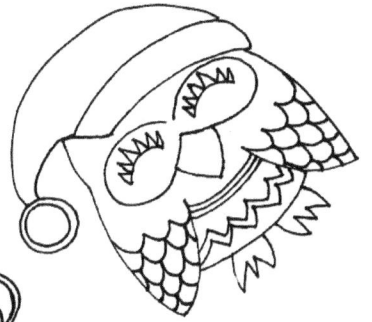

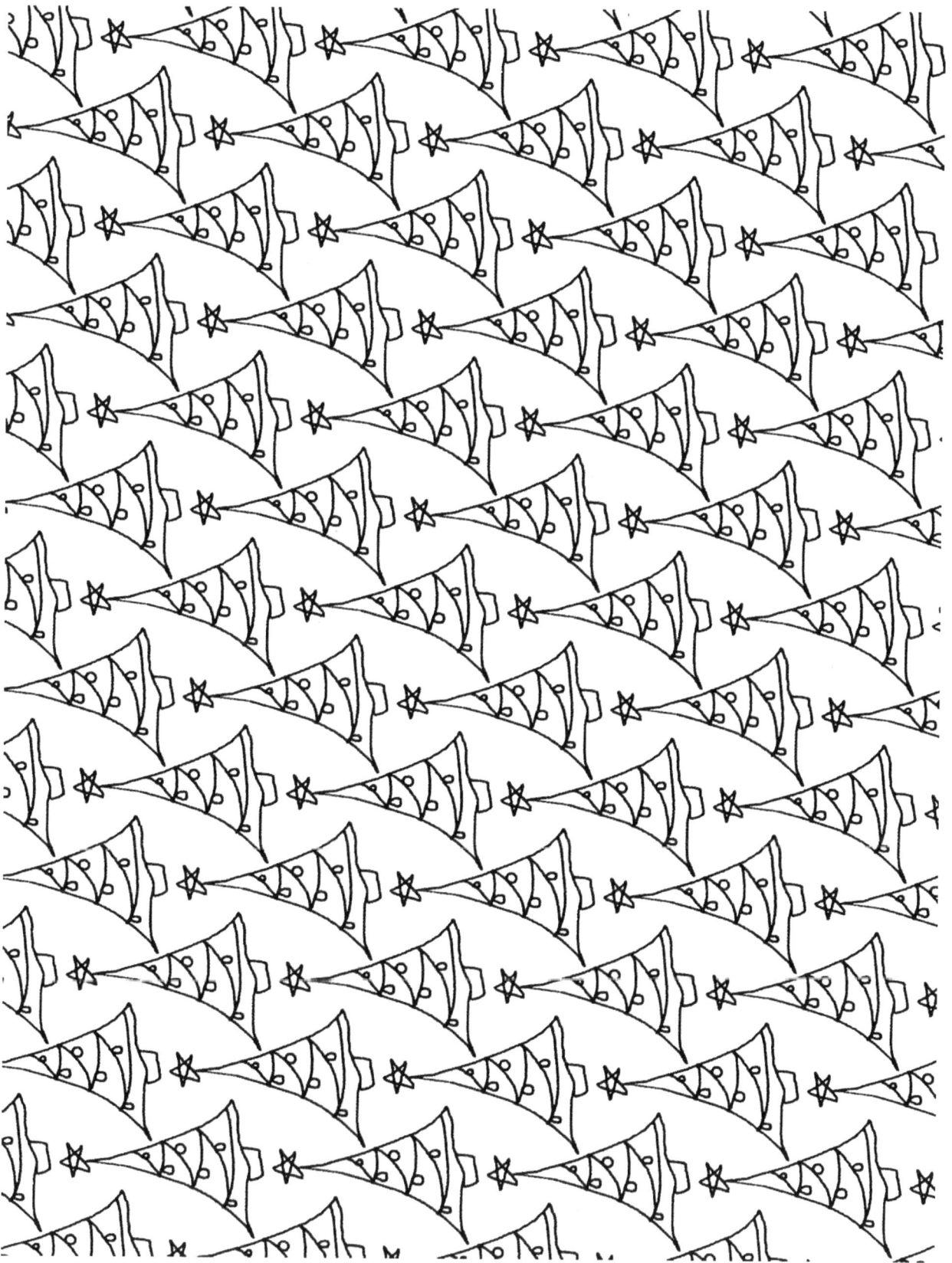

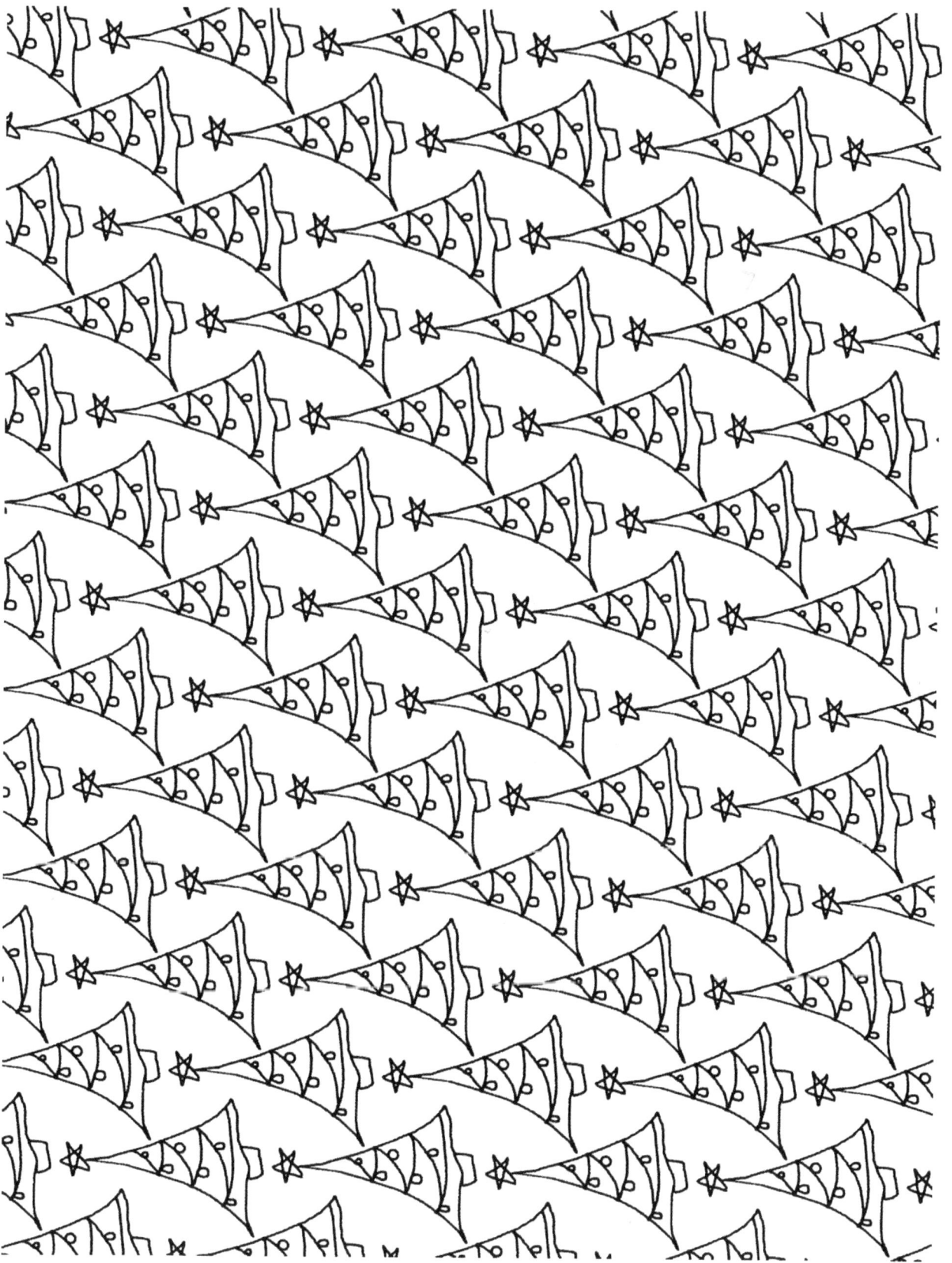

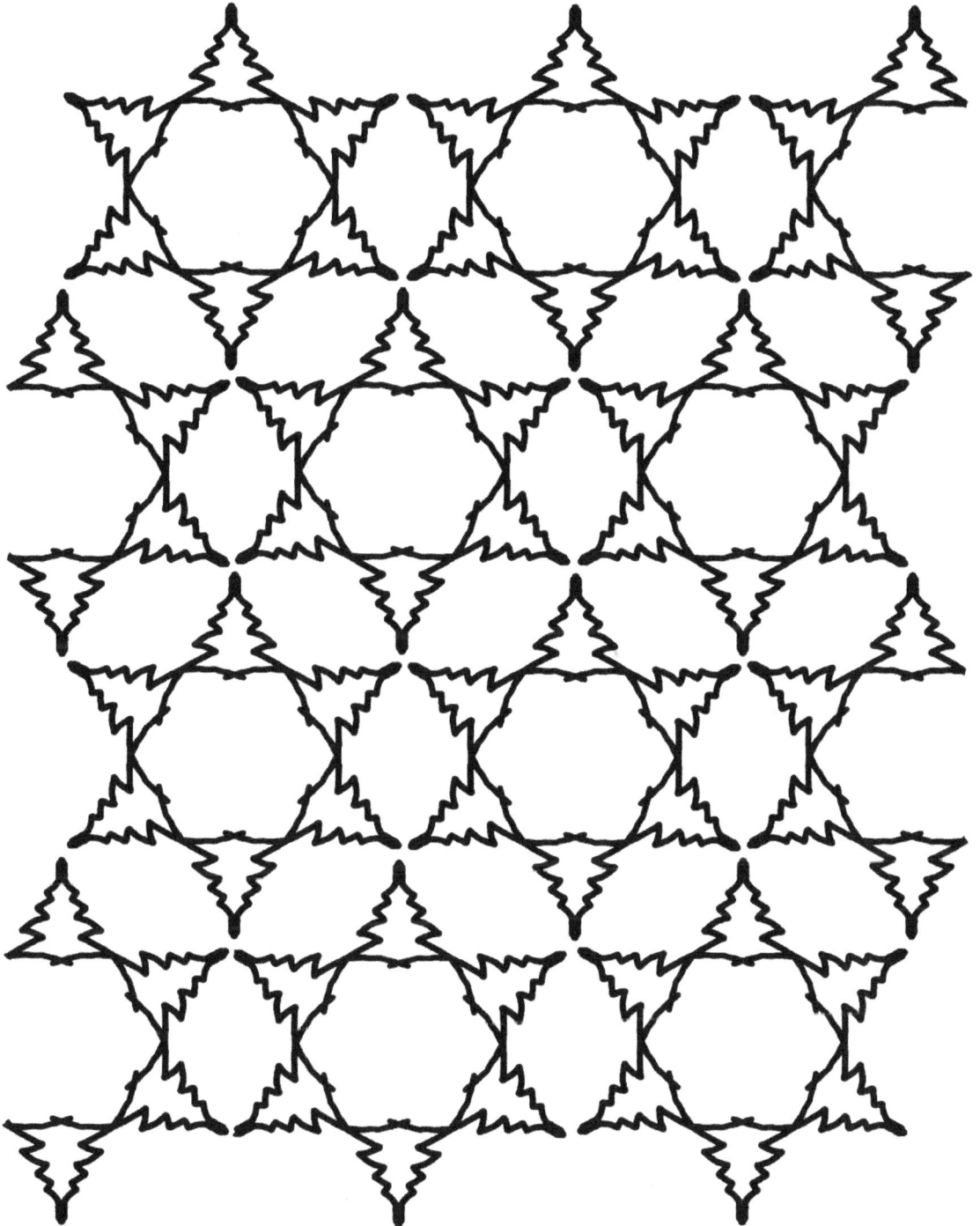

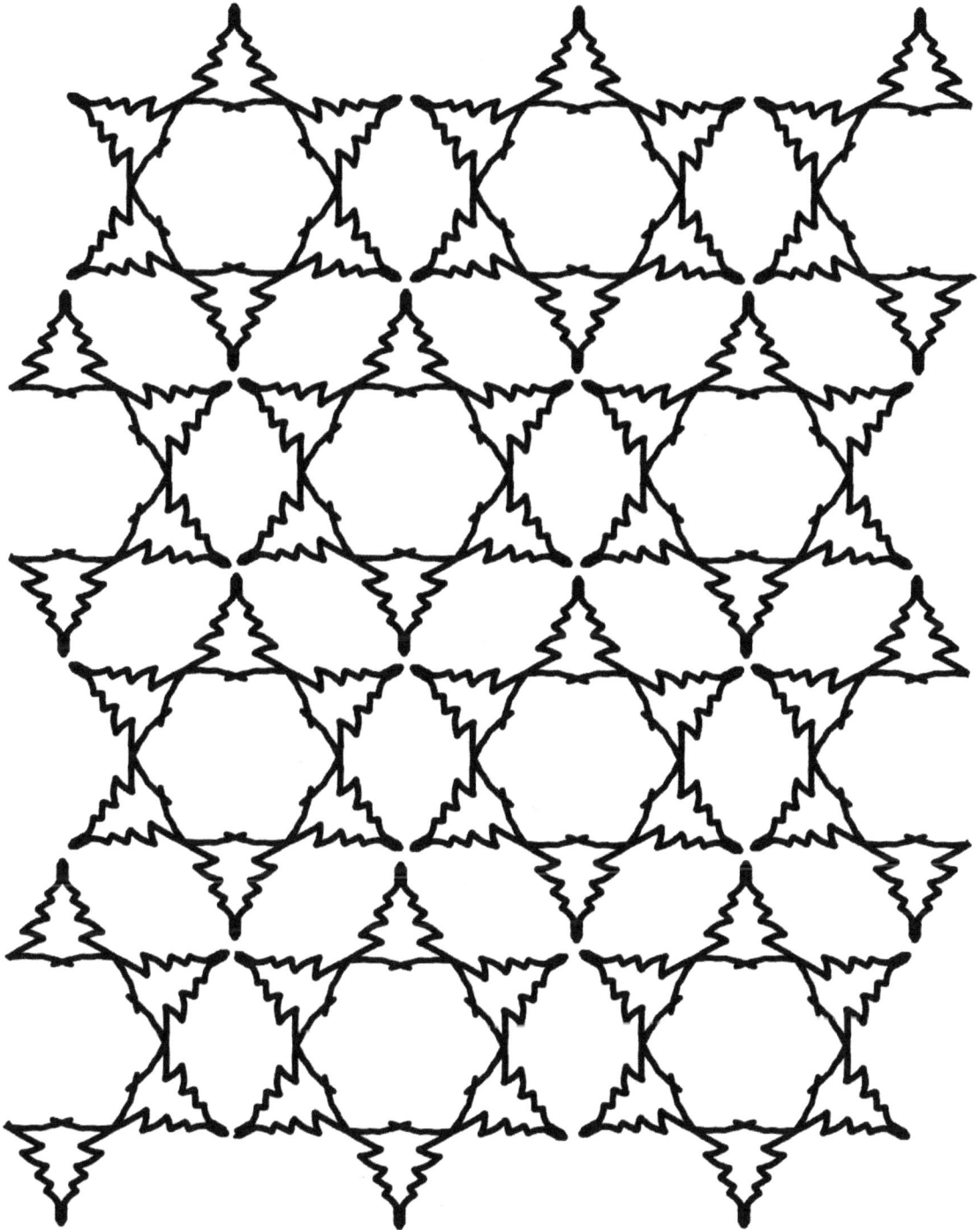

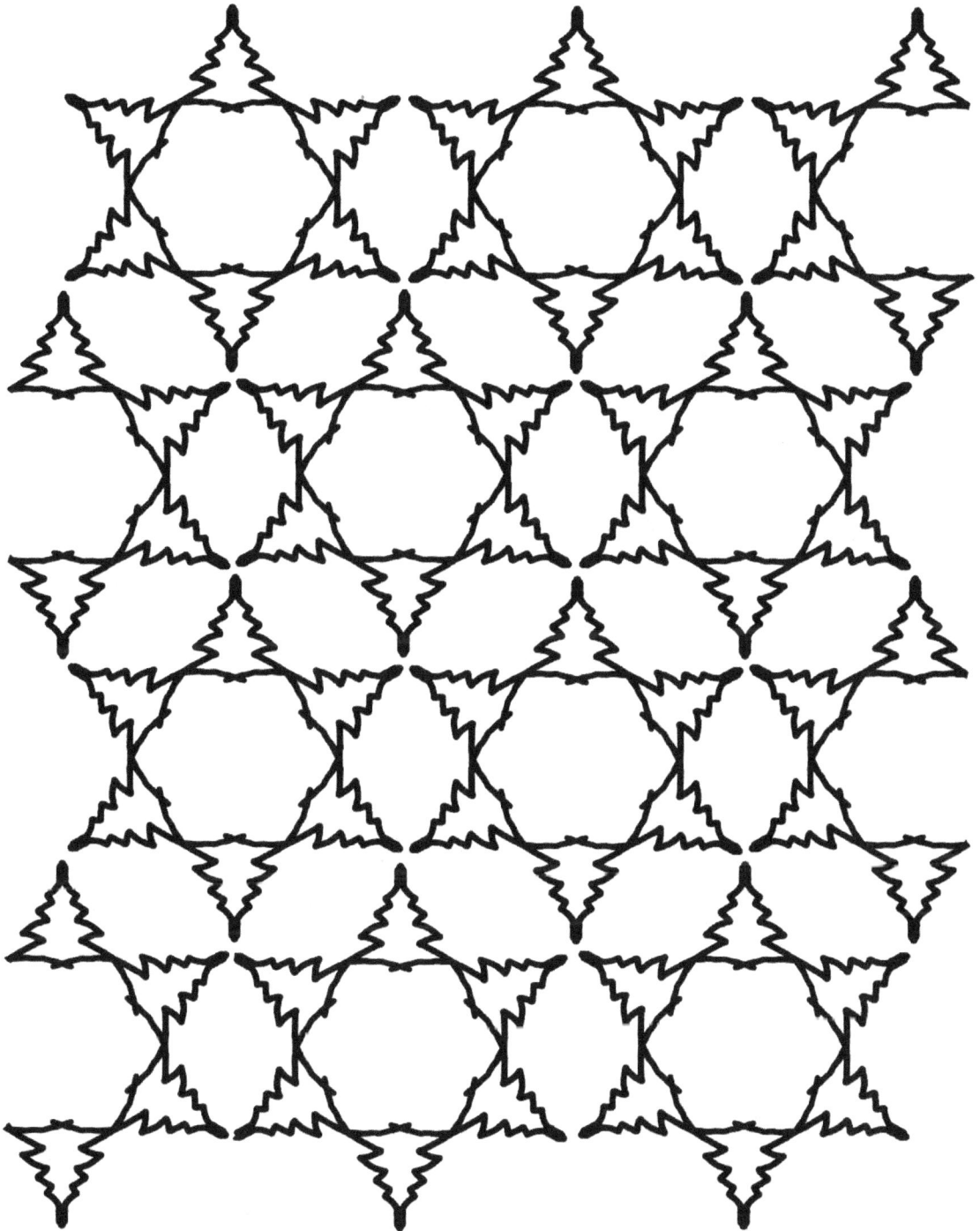

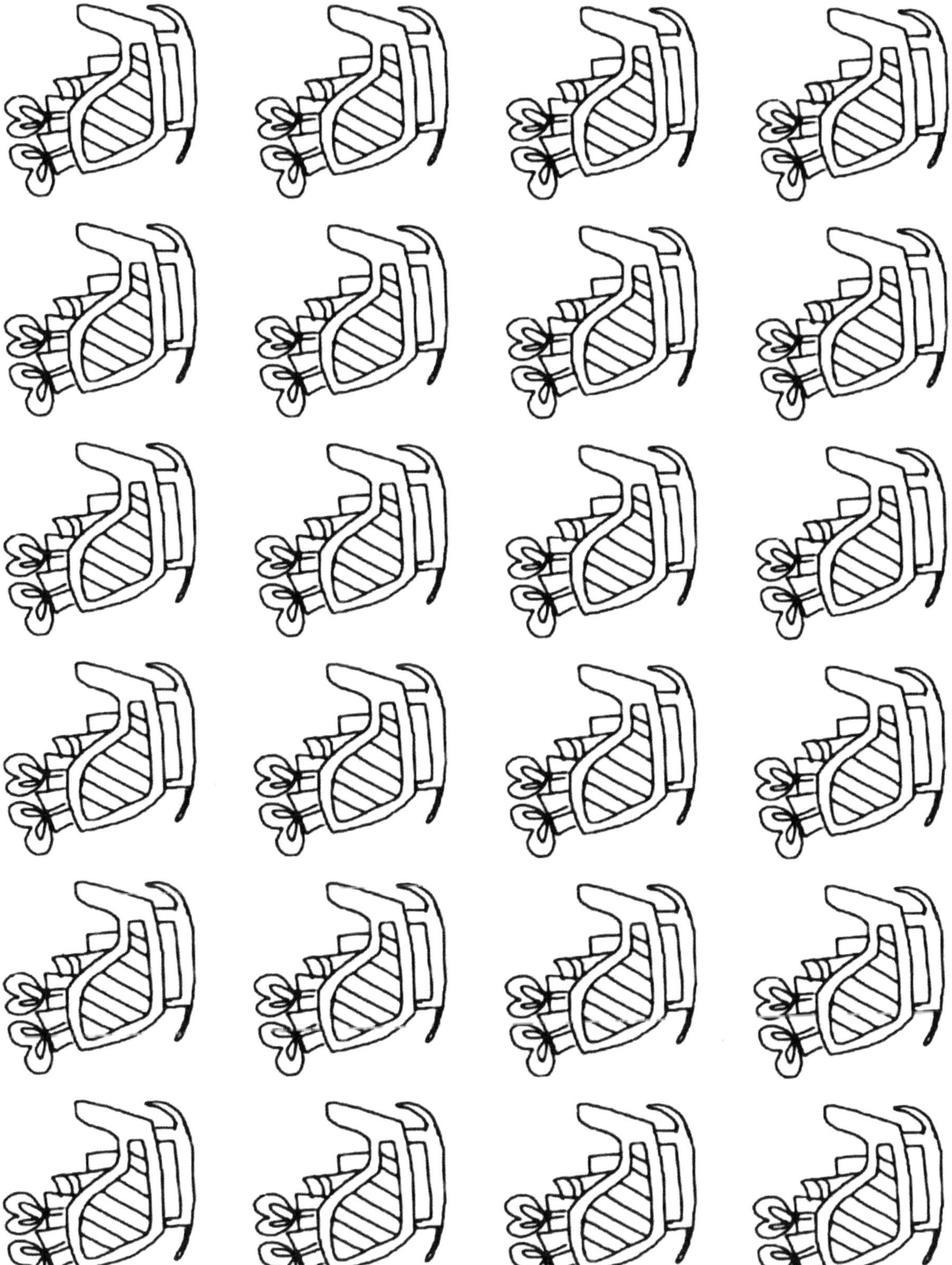

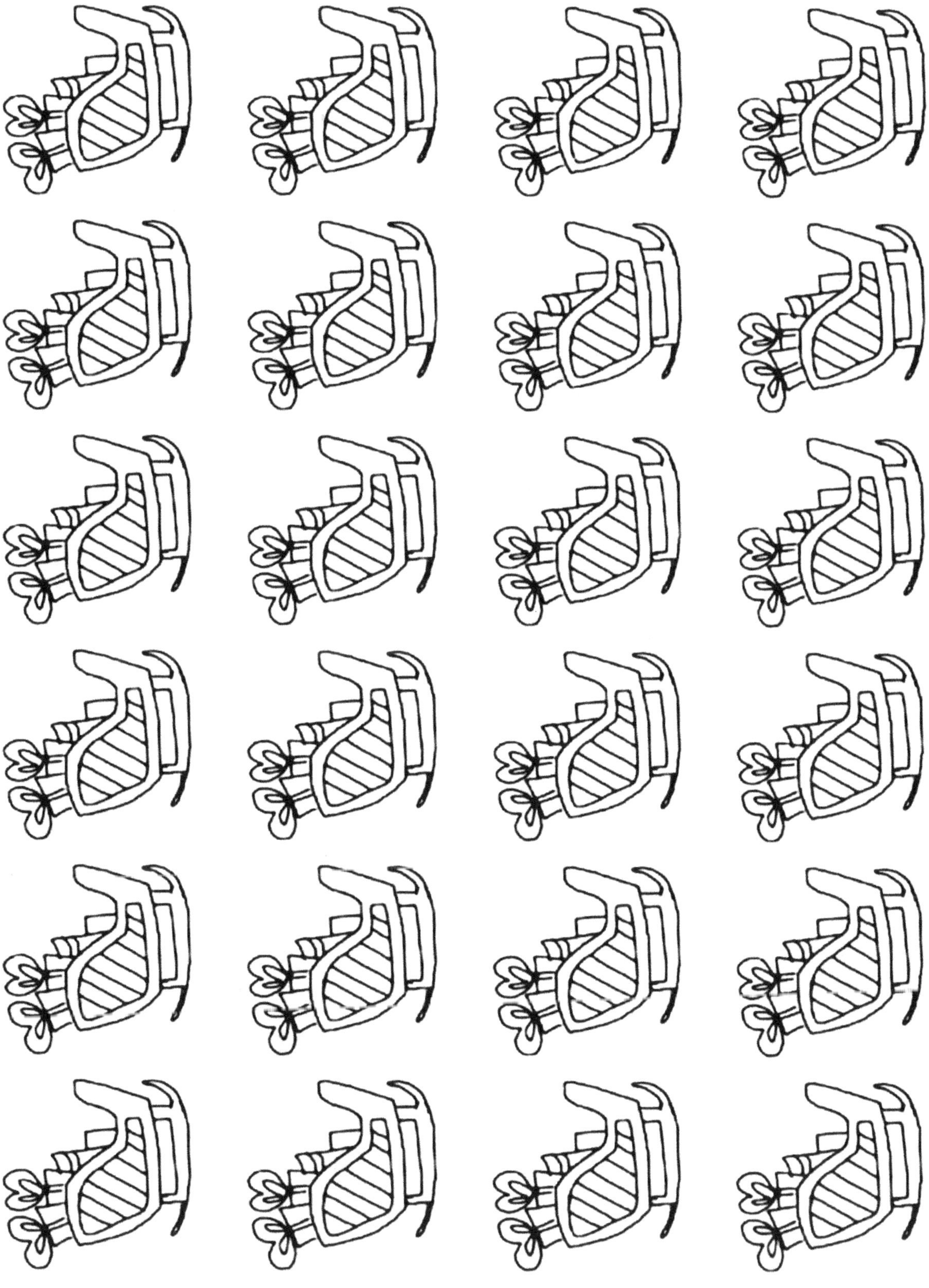

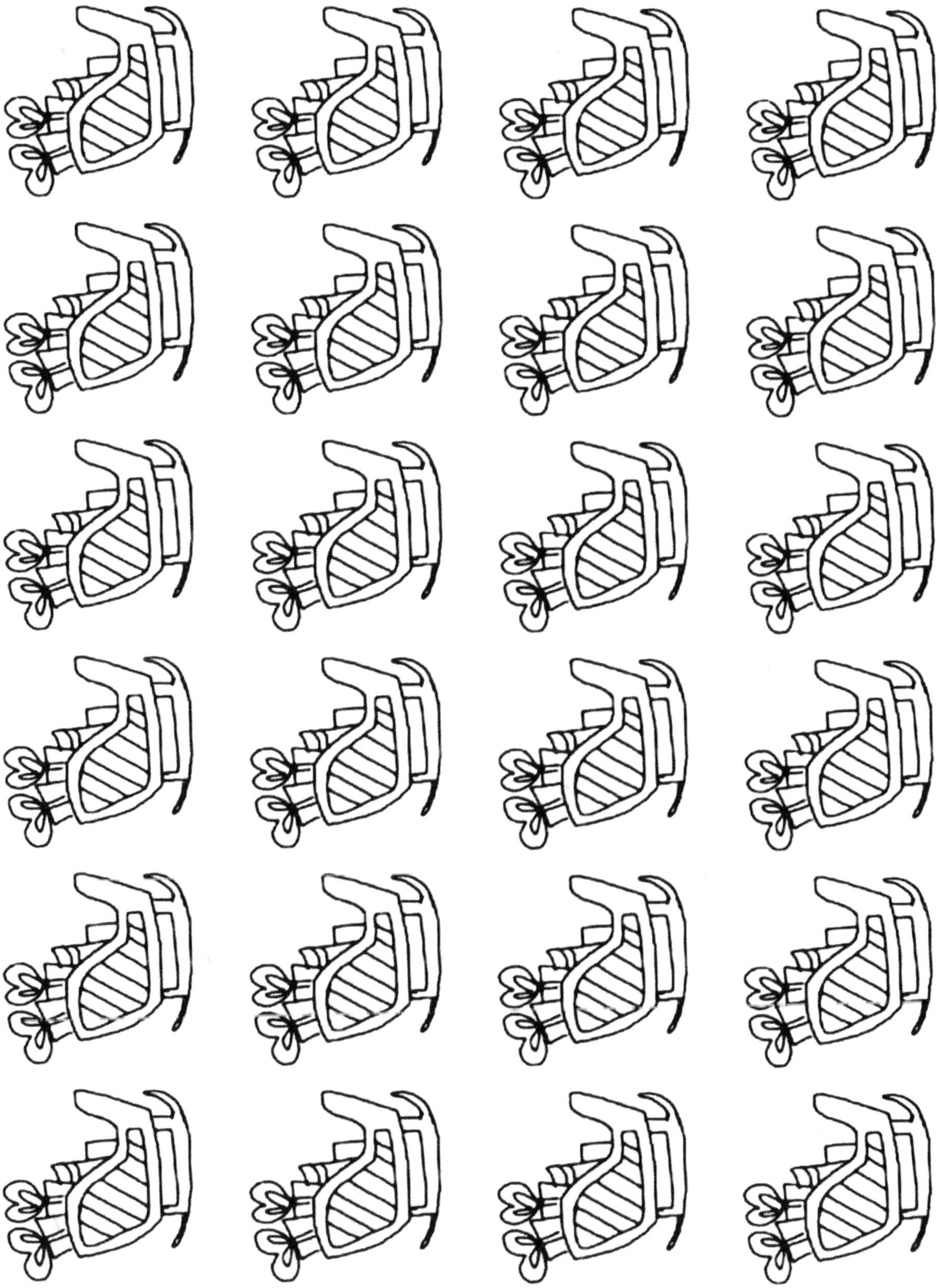

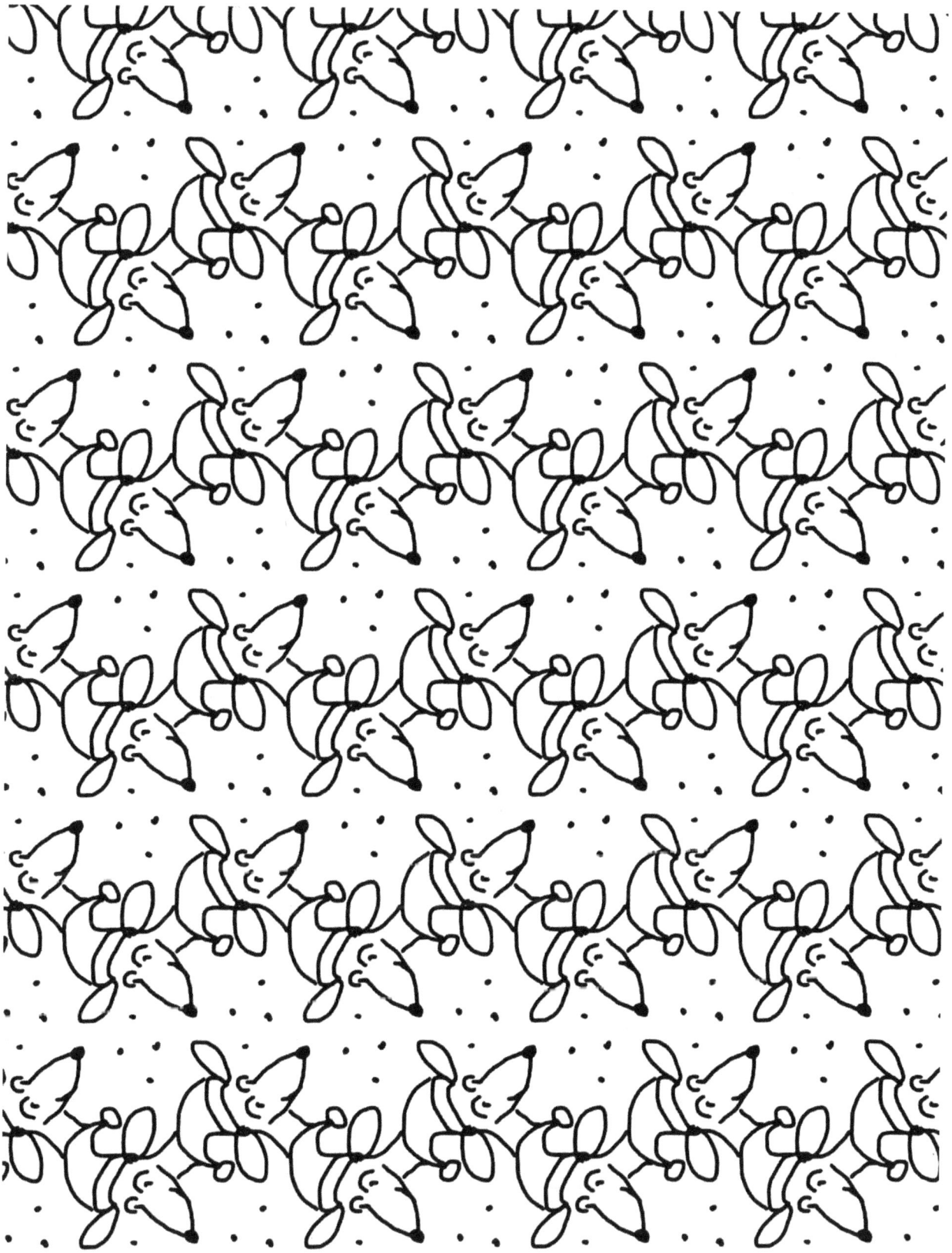

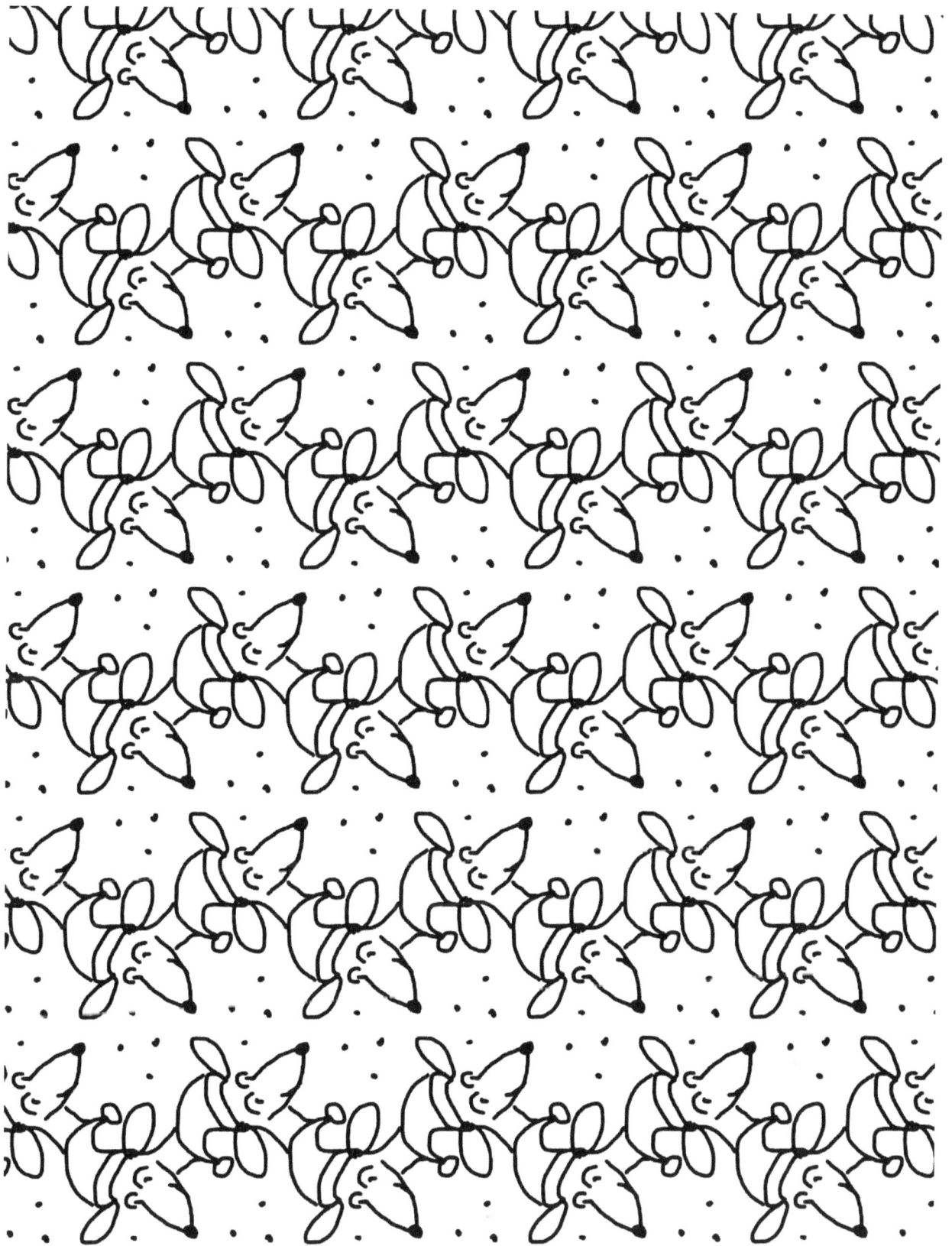

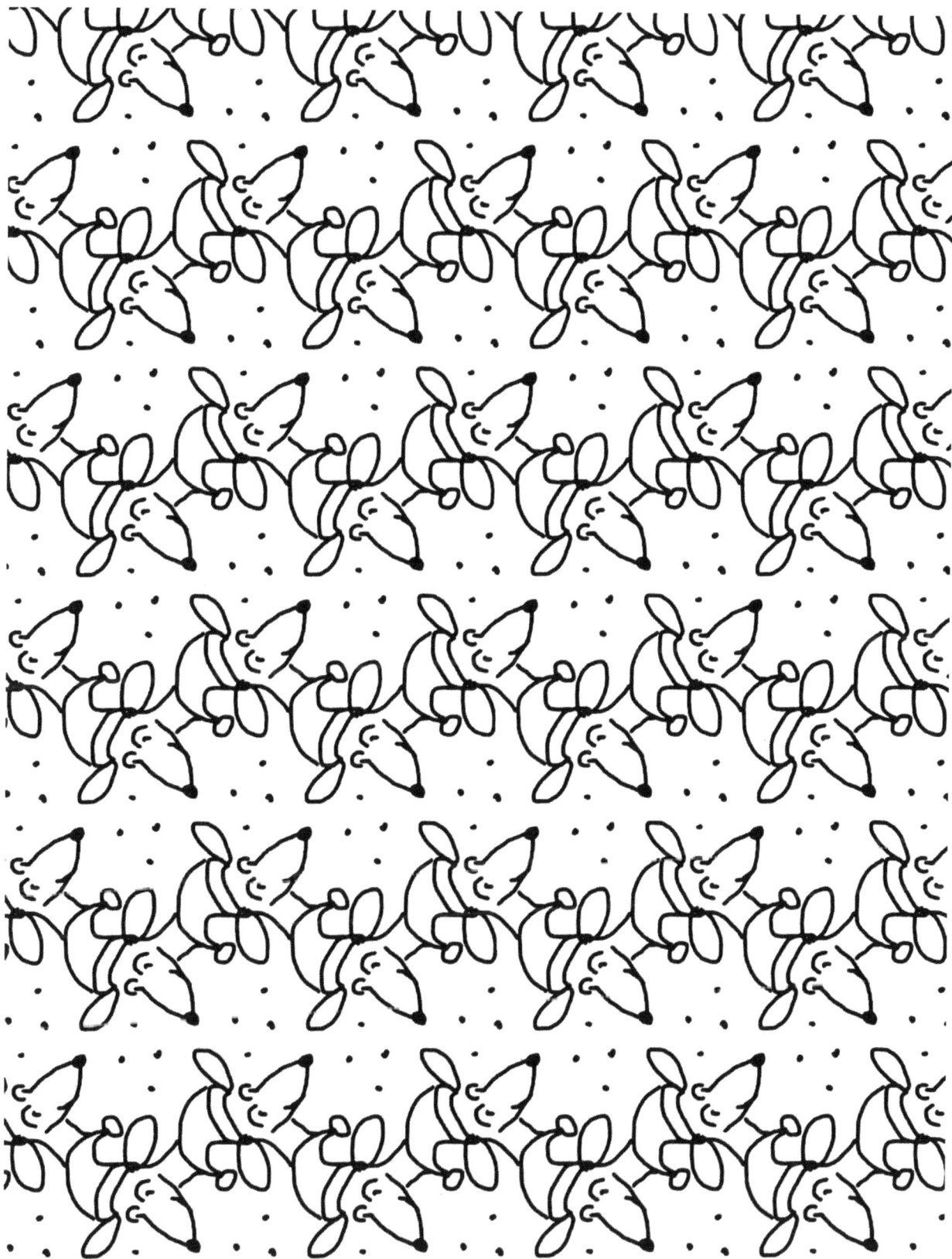

Are you coloring with pens?

Be careful that you don't get ink
from the back of your page
onto the next page.

Tear out these blank pages
and place them behind the sheet
you are coloring on, just in case.

Enjoy your time
coloring together!

I wish you a very merry Christmas
full of peace, joy, and wonder.

Visit our website at Coloring Camelot.com
to find more images!

Suzanna Stinnett
California 2015

www.ingramcontent.com/pod-product-compliance
Lightning Source LLC
Chambersburg PA
CBHW080520030426
42337CB00023B/4582